SYLLABUS STD 10

YEARLY PLANNER FOR ACADEMIC YEAR 2022-23

AASHISH

Copyright © Aashish
All Rights Reserved.

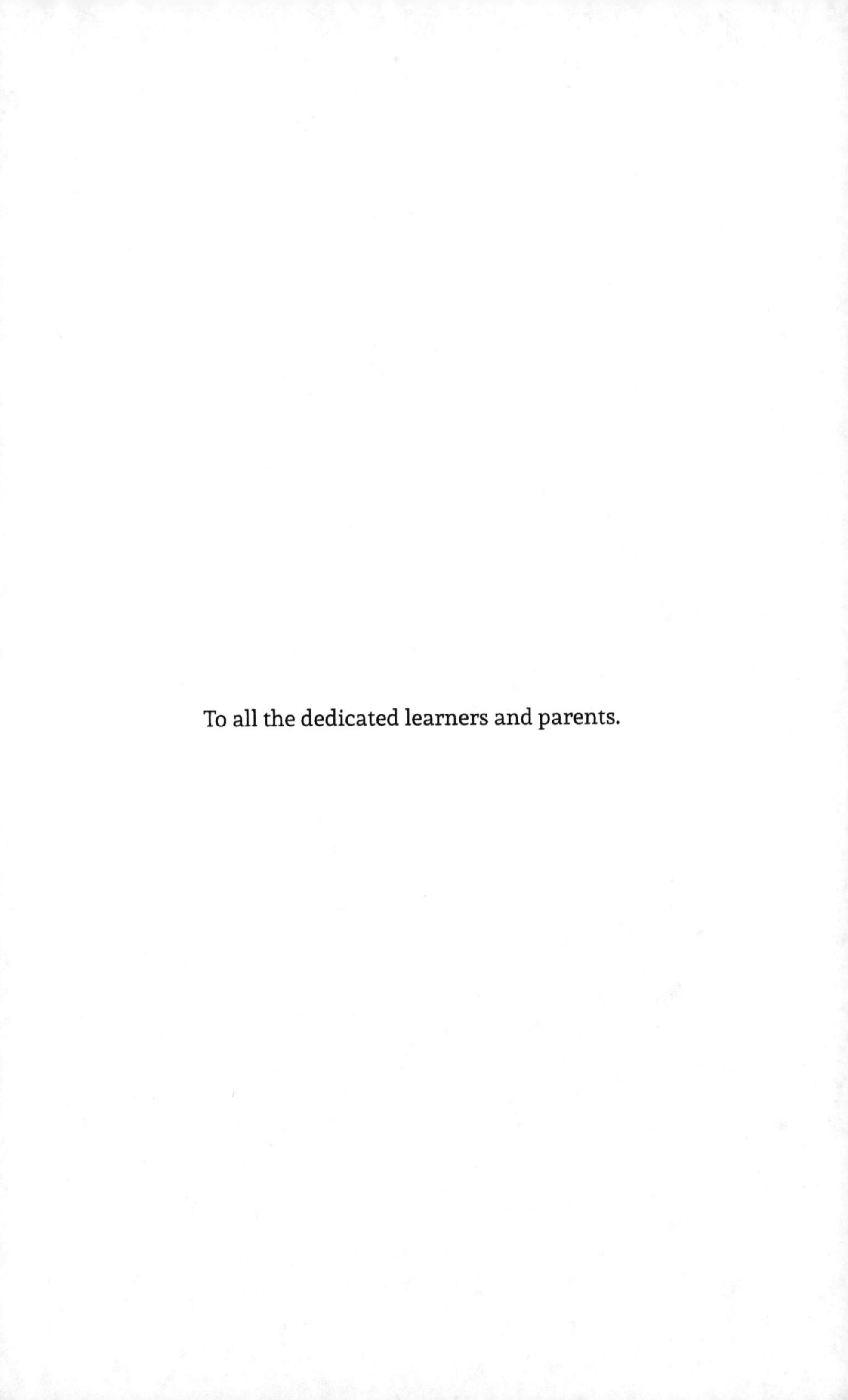
To all the dedicated learners and parents.

Contents

Foreword

I believe that education shapes the character, calibre and prospect of an individual. Education has no perimeter to restrict. Intensive and critical thinking, sharpening intelligence, refining character — all are a part of dignified education. Students of Heavenly Blessings Academy are benefitted by such type of education.

Preface

This book contains complete syllabus for Class 10 CBSE for the subjects of English, Mathematics, Science and Social Science. It also contains paper patterns and Marks wise weightage for every lesson of all the subjects.

Yearly planner is also mentioned at last.

Few additional activities that will be conducted this year: I-IBPL Season 3: Box Cricket Tournament.

Movie Time.

Trek Trip: If things go well with permissions.

Academic Competitions: Elocution, Debate, *etc.*

Book Writing Activity.

This year we would also provide extra books 'FIB Spotlight' that will contain summarised lessons in lucid language, solutions to INERT Textual Questions, Extra Important Mark wise Questions, Important MC Q and lots more.

Why to *select* us?

Because all the costs are included in the fees and no extra cost will be
incurred! Neither for the Andriod Application or for the Extra Books, Activities, Tests, Trips, Practicals, ID cards, etc. etc. etc.

Acknowledgements

Special Thanks to my team of learners, motivators, friends, parents and Team Heavenly Blessings.

Prologue

My Goals This Year:

I will help to create a shared vision for students, staff and community members. I will take the time to gather input and knowledge from as many stakeholders as possible.

I will utilize my supervisory time to build and establish relationships with students and staff. I will talk with students and staff and ask them about their lives in a sincere and caring manner. I will take an active interest in learning as much as I can about them. I will have high expectations for students, staff and myself. I will help to empower others to take control of their own learning and development by establishing an environment built on accountability and responsibility.

I will support and encourage those with whom I work. I will work to embrace a sharing and collaborative school culture that takes risks in an effort to do great things.

I will listen more than I talk. I will use my two ears more than I use my one mouth, and I will try to learn as much as I can from others. I will make it a priority to get into classrooms to observe on a daily basis, and I will learn by listening and observing.

I will communicate with and involve parents and community stakeholders as often as possible. I will work with teachers and staff to keep parents informed and up-to-date with what is going on in our school through the use of weekly newsletters, our school website and social media outlets.

I will share the power of my PLN with my colleagues. I will take the time to meet with anyone interested in learning more about using social media as a means toward professional growth. I willmodel being a lifelong learner for both students and staff. I will have a healthy balance between my professional and personal life. Though I anticipate the high level of time commitment required for this job, I do not want my job to consume my entire life. My family, friends and colleagues will all benefit from this healthy balance.

I will base every decision I make on what is best for students. It is difficult to not get caught up in everything that is going on, but I will make every effort to put students and their needs first.

ONE
ENGLISH SYLLABUS TERM I

Course Structure for CBSE Class 10 English (Code No. 184) First Term

Section	Weightage (in Marks)
Reading	10
Writing and Grammar	10
Literature	20
Total	40
Internal Assessment	10
Grand Total	50

COURSE STRUCTURE TERM I

READING

Question based on the following kinds of unseen passages to assess inference, evaluation, vocabulary, analysis and interpretation:

1. Discursive passage (400-450 words)
2. Case based Factual passage (with visual input/ statistical data/ chart etc. 300-350

words)

WRITING SKILL

1. Formal letter based on a given situation.
→ Letter to the Editor
→ Letter of Complaint (Official)
→ Letter of Complaint (Business)

GRAMMAR

1. Tenses
2. Modals
3. Subject-Verb Concord
4. Determiner
5. Reported Speech
6. Commands and Requests
7. Statements
8. Questions

LITERATURE

Questions based on extracts / texts to assess interpretation, inference, extrapolation beyond

the text and across the texts.

FIRST FLIGHT

1. A Letter to God
2. Nelson Mandela
3. Two Stories About Flying
4. From the Diary of Anne Frank
5. The Hundred Dresses 1
6. The Hundred Dresses 2

POEMS

1. Dust of Snow
2. Fire and Ice

TWO

MATHEMATICS SYLLABUS TERM I

CBSE Class 10 Maths Revised/Rationalised Syllabus for Term 1:

No.	Unit Name	Marks
I	NUMBER SYSTEMS	6
II	ALGEBRA	10
III	COORDINATE GEOMETRY	6
IV	GEOMETRY	6
V	TRIGONOMETRY	5
VI	MENSURATION	4
VII	STATISTICS & PROBABILITY	3
	Total	40
	Internal Assessment	10
	Total	50

COURSE STRUCTURE TERM I

Components of IA	Marks	Total Marks
Periodic Test	3	
Multiple Assessments	2	
Portfolio	2	10 marks for the term
Student Enrichment Activities-practical work	3	

INTERNAL ASSESSMENT TERM I

UNIT-NUMBER SYSTEMS
1.REAL NUMBER

Fundamental Theorem of Arithmetic - statements after reviewing work done earlier and after illustrating and motivating through examples. Decimal representation of rational numbers in terms of terminating/non-terminating recurring decimals.

UNIT-ALGEBRA
2.POLYNOMIALS

Zeroes of a polynomial. Relationship between zeroes and coefficients of quadratic polynomials only.

3.PAIR OF LINEAR EQUATIONS IN TWO VARIABLES

Pair of linear equations in two variables and graphical method of their solution, consistency/inconsistency. Algebraic conditions for number of solutions. Solution of a pair of linear equations in two variables algebraically - by substitution and by elimination. Simple situational problems. Simple problems on equations reducible to linear equations.

UNIT-COORDINATE GEOMETRY
4.COORDINATE GEOMETRY

LINES (In two-dimensions)

Review: Concepts of coordinate geometry, graphs of linear equations. Distance formula. Section formula (internal division)

UNIT-GEOMETRY

5.TRIANGLES

Definitions, examples, counter examples of similar triangles.

1. (Prove) If a line is drawn parallel to one side of a triangle to intersect the other two sides in distinct points, the other two sides are divided in the same ratio.

2. (Motivate) If a line divides two sides of a triangle in the same ratio, the line is parallel to the third side.

3. (Motivate) If in two triangles, the corresponding angles are equal, their corresponding sides are proportional and the triangles are similar.

4. (Motivate) If the corresponding sides of two triangles are proportional, their corresponding angles are equal and the two triangles are similar.

5. (Motivate) If one angle of a triangle is equal to one angle of another triangle and the sides including these angles are proportional, the two triangles are similar.

6. (Motivate) If a perpendicular is drawn from the vertex of the right angle of a right triangle to the hypotenuse, the triangles on each side of the perpendicular are similar to the whole triangle and to each other.

7. (Motivate) The ratio of the areas of two similar triangles is equal to the ratio of the squares of their corresponding sides.

8. (Prove) In a right triangle, the square on the hypotenuse is equal to the sum of the squares on the other two sides.

9. (Motivate) In a triangle, if the square on one side is equal to sum of the squares on the other two sides, the angle opposite to the first side is a right angle.

UNIT- TRIGONOMETRY

6.INTRODUCTION TO TRIGONOMETRY

Trigonometric ratios of an acute angle of a right-angled triangle. Proof of their existence (well defined). Values of the trigonometric ratios of 300 , 450 and 600 . Relationships between the ratios.

TRIGONOMETRIC IDENTITIES

Proof and applications of the identity sin2A + cos2A = 1. Only simple identities to be given

UNIT-MENSURATION

7.AREAS RELATED TO CIRCLES

Motivate the area of a circle; area of sectors and segments of a circle. Problems based on areas and perimeter / circumference of the above said plane figures. (In calculating area of segment of a circle, problems should be restricted to central angle of 60° and 90° only. Plane figures involving triangles, simple quadrilaterals and circle should be taken.)

UNIT- STATISTICS & PROBABILITY

8.PROBABILITY

Classical definition of probability. Simple problems on finding the probability of an event.

FOR MATHEMATICS, STUDENTS WILL ALSO BE PROVIDED WITH NCERT EXEMPLAR.

THREE

SCIENCE SYLLABUS TERM I

General Instructions:

1. The total Theory Examinations (Term I+II) will be of 80 marks and 20 marks weightage shall be for Internal Assessment (Term I+II).

2. Internal Assessment - Maximum Marks 10 for each Term:

a. There will be Periodic Assessment that would include:

· Three periodic tests will be conducted by the school in the entire session. Average of the two periodic tests/marks of best periodic Test conducted in the Term is to be taken for consideration.

· Diverse methods of assessment as per the need of the class dynamics and curriculum transaction. These may include - short tests, oral test, quiz, concept maps, projects, posters, presentations, enquiry based scientific investigations etc.

b. Subject Enrichment in the form of Practical/Laboratory work should be done throughout the year and the student should maintain record of the same. Practical Assessment should be continuous. All practicals listed in the syllabus must be completed.

c. Portfolio to be prepared by the student- This would include class work and other sample of student work.

Course Structure for CBSE Class 10 Science First Term

Units		Marks
I	Chemical Substances-Nature and Behaviour: Chapter 1, 2 and 3	16
II	World of Living: Chapter 6	10
III	Natural Phenomena: Chapter 10 and 11	14
	Total	40
	Internal Assessment	10
	Total	50

COURSE STRUCTURE TERM I

Theme: Materials
Unit I: Chemical Substances - Nature and Behaviour
Chapter - 1 Chemical reactions and equations

Chemical reactions: Chemical equation, Balanced chemical equation, implications of a balanced chemical equation, types of chemical reactions: combination, decomposition, displacement, double displacement, precipitation, neutralization, oxidation and reduction.

Chapter - 2 Acids, Bases and Salts

Acids, bases and salts: Their definitions in terms of furnishing of H+ and OHions, General properties, examples and uses, concept of pH scale (Definition relating to logarithm not required), importance of pH in everyday life; preparation and uses of Sodium Hydroxide, Bleaching powder, Baking soda, Washing soda and Plaster of Paris.

Chapter - 3 Metals and non-metals

Metals and nonmetals: Properties of metals and non-metals; Reactivity series; Formation and properties of ionic compounds.

Theme: The World of the Living
Unit II: World of Living
Chapter - 6 Life processes
Life processes: 'Living Being'. Basic concept of nutrition, respiration, transport and excretion in plants and animals.
Theme: How Things Work
Unit III: Natural Phenomena
Chapter - 10 Light - Reflection and Refraction
Reflection of light by curved surfaces; Images formed by spherical mirrors, centre of curvature, principal axis, principal focus, focal length, mirror formula (Derivation not required), magnification.
Refraction; Laws of refraction, refractive index.
Refraction of light by spherical lens; Image formed by spherical lenses; Lens formula (Derivation not required); Magnification.
Power of a lens.
Chapter - 11 Human eye and colourful world
Refraction of light through a prism, dispersion of light, scattering of light, applications in daily life.
PRACTICALS
Practical should be conducted alongside the concepts taught in theory classes.
TERM-I
LIST OF EXPERIMENTS
1. A. Finding the pH of the following samples by using pH paper/ universal indicator:
(i) Dilute Hydrochloric Acid
(ii) Dilute NaOH solution
(iii) Dilute Ethanoic Acid solution
(iv) Lemon juice
(v) Water
(vi) Dilute Hydrogen Carbonate solution
B. Studying the properties of acids and bases (HCl & NaOH) on the basis of their reaction with:
a) Litmus solution (Blue/Red)

b) Zinc metal

c) Solid sodium carbonate Unit–I:(Chapter-2)

2. Performing and observing the following reactions and classifying them into:

A.Combination reaction B. Decomposition reaction C. Displacement reaction D. Double displacement reaction

(i) Action of water on quicklime

(ii) Action of heat on ferrous sulphate crystals

(iii) Iron nails kept in copper sulphate solution

(iv) Reaction between sodium sulphate and barium chloride solutions. Unit-I:(Chapter-1)

3. A. Observing the action of Zn, Fe, Cu and Al metals on the following salt solutions:

(i) $ZnSO_4$(aq)

(ii) $FeSO_4$(aq)

(iii)$CuSO_4$(aq)

(iv)$Al_2(SO_4)_3$(aq)

B. Arranging Zn, Fe, Cu and Al (metals) in the decreasing order of reactivity based on the above result. Unit-I :(Chapter-3)

4. Experimentally show that carbon dioxide is given out during respiration. Unit-II:(Chapter-6)

5. Determination of the focal length of (i) Concave mirror and (ii) Convex lens by obtaining the image of a distant object. Unit-III:(Chapter- 10)

6. Tracing the path of a ray of light passing through a rectangular glass slab for different angles of incidence. Measure the angle of incidence, angle of refraction, angle of emergence and interpret the result. Unit-III:(Chapter-10)

7. Tracing the path of the rays of light through a glass prism. Unit-III:(Chapter-11)

Competencies	Marks
Demonstrate Knowledge and Understanding	46%
Application of Knowledge/Concepts	22%
Analyze, Evaluate and Create	32%

Assessment Areas (Theory)

Internal Assessment – Total 10 Marks
➤ Periodic Assessment - 03 marks
➤ Multiple Assessment - 02 marks
➤ Subject Enrichment (Practical Work) - 03 marks
➤ Portfolio - 02 marks

FOUR

SOCIAL SCIENCE SYLLABUS TERM I

Course Structure - Class 10th Social Science Term 1

No.	Units	No. of Periods	Marks
I	India and the Contemporary World -1	12	10
II	Contemporary India – I	16	10
III	Democratic Politics – I	14	10
IV	Economics	20	10
	Total	62	40

Course Structure - Class 10th Social Science Term 1

COURSE CONTENT - Class 10th Term 1
TERM- I
  Unit 1: India and the Contemporary World – II
Section 1: Events and Processes

1. The Rise of Nationalism in Europe

- The French Revolution and the Idea of the Nation
- The Making of Nationalism in Europe
- The Age of Revolutions: 1830-1848
- The Making of Germany and Italy
- Visualizing the Nation
- Nationalism and Imperialism

Unit 2: Contemporary India – II

1. Resources and Development

- Types of Resources
- Development of Resources
- Resource Planning in India
- Land Resources
- Land Utilization
- Land Use Pattern in India
- Land Degradation and Conservation Measures
- Soil as a Resource
- Classification of Soils
- Soil Erosion and Soil Conservation

3. Water Resources

- Water Scarcity and The Need for Water Conservation and Management
- Multi-Purpose River Projects and Integrated Water Resources Management
- Rainwater Harvesting

Note: The theoretical aspect of chapter 'Water Resources' to be assessed in the Periodic Tests only and will not be evaluated in Board Examination. However, the map items of this chapter as listed will be evaluated in Board Examination.

4. Agriculture

- Types of farming
- Cropping Pattern
- Major Crops
- Technological and Institutional Reforms
- Impact of Globalization on Agriculture

Unit 3: Democratic Politics – II

1. Power Sharing

- Case Studies of Belgium and Sri Lanka
- Why power sharing is desirable?
- Forms of Power Sharing

2. Federalism

- What is Federalism?
- What make India a Federal Country?
- How is Federalism practiced?
- Decentralization in India

Unit 4: Economics

1. Development

- What Development Promises - Different people different goals
- Income and other goals
- National Development
- How to compare different countries or states?
- Income and other criteria
- Public Facilities
- Sustainability of development

2. Sectors of the Indian Economy

- Sectors of Economic Activities
- Comparing the three sectors
- Primary, Secondary and Tertiary Sectors in India
- Division of sectors as organized and unorganized
- Sectors in terms of ownership: Public and Private Sectors

LIST OF MAP ITEMS CLASS X TERM – I

A.GEOGRAPHY

Chapter 1: Resources and Development

a. Major soil Types Chapter

3: Water Resources

Dams:

a. Salal

b. Bhakra Nangal

c. Tehri

d. Rana Pratap Sagar

e. Sardar Sarovar

f. Hirakud

g. Nagarjuna Sagar

h. Tungabhadra

Note: The theoretical aspect of chapter 'Water Resources' to be assessed in the Periodic Tests only and will not be evaluated in Board Examination. However, the map items of this chapter as listed above will be evaluated in Board Examination.

Chapter 4: Agriculture

a. Major areas of Rice and Wheat

b. Largest / Major producer States of Sugarcane, Tea, Coffee, Rubber, Cotton and Jute

Internal Assessment:

	Marks	Description
Periodic Assessment	10 Marks	<table><tr><td>Pen Paper Test</td><td>**5 marks**</td></tr><tr><td>Assessment using multiple strategies For example, Quiz, Debate, Role Play, Viva, Group Discussion, Visual Expression, Interactive Bulletin Boards, Gallery Walks, Exit Cards, Concept Maps, Peer Assessment, Self-Assessment, etc.</td><td>**5 marks**</td></tr></table>
Portfolio	5 Marks	• Classwork and Assignments • Any exemplary work done by the student • Reflections, Narrations, Journals, etc. • Achievements of the student in the subject throughout the year • Participation of the student in different activities like Heritage India Quiz
Subject Enrichment Activity	5 Marks	• Project Work
TOTAL	**20 MARKS**	

PROJECT WORK

05 Marks

1. Every student has to compulsorily undertake any one project on the following topics: Consumer Awareness OR Social Issues
OR
Sustainable Development

2. Objective: The overall objective of the project work is to help students gain an insight and pragmatic understanding of the theme and see all the Social Science disciplines from interdisciplinary perspective. It should also help in enhancing the Life Skills of the students.

Students are expected to apply the Social Science concepts that they have learnt over the years in order to prepare the project report.

If required, students may go out for collecting data and use different primary and secondary resources to prepare the project. If possible, different forms of Art may be integrated in the project work.

3. The distribution of marks over different aspects relating to Project Work is as follows:

S. No.	Aspects	Marks
a.	Content accuracy, originality and analysis	2
b.	Presentation and creativity	2
c.	Viva Voce	1

PROJECT ASSESSMENT

4. The projects carried out by the students in different topics should subsequently be shared among themselves through interactive sessions such as exhibitions, panel discussions, etc.

5. All documents pertaining to assessment under this activity should be meticulously maintained by concerned schools.

6. A Summary Report should be prepared highlighting:

→ objectives realized through individual work and group interactions;

→ calendar of activities;

→ innovative ideas generated in the process (like comic strips, drawings, illustrations, script play etc.);

→ list of questions asked in viva voce.

7. It is to be noted here by all the teachers and students that the projects and models prepared should be made from eco-friendly products without incurring too much expenditure.

8. The Project Report should be handwritten by the students themselves.

9. Records pertaining to projects (internal assessment) of the students will be maintained for a period of three months from the date of declaration of result for verification at the discretion of Board. Subjudiced cases, if any or those involving RTI / Grievances may however be retained beyond three months.

FIVE

ENGLISH SYLLABUS TERM II

CBSE Class 10 English Syllabus (Code No. 184) Term 2

Section	Weightage (in Marks)
Reading	10
Writing and Grammar	10
Literature	20
Total	40
Internal Assessment	10
Grand Total	50

COURSE STRUCTURE TERM I

READING

Questions based on the following kinds of unseen passages to assess inference, evaluation, vocabulary, analysis and interpretation:

1. Discursive passage (400-450 words)

2. Case based Factual passage (with visual input/ statistical data/ chart etc. 300-350 words)

WRITING SKILL

1. Formal letter based on a given situation ·

Letter of Order

Letter of Enquiry

2. Analytical Paragraph (based on outline/chart/cue/map/report etc.)

GRAMMAR

1. Tenses

2. Modals

3. Subject Verb Concord

4. Determiner

5. Reported Speech

6. Commands and Requests

7. Statements

8. Questions

LITERATURE

Questions based on extracts / texts to assess interpretation, inference, extrapolation beyond the text and across the texts.

FIRST FLIGHT

1. Glimpses of India

2. Madam Rides the Bus

3. The Sermon at Benares

4. The Proposal (Play)

POEMS

1. Amanda

2. Animals

3. The Tale of Custard the Dragon

FOOTPRINTS WITHOUT FEET

1. The Making of a Scientist

2. The Necklace
3. The Hack Driver
4. Bholi

SIX

MATHEMATICS SYLLABUS TERM II

COURSE STRUCTURE CLASS 10th (2021-22) SECOND TERM

No.	Unit Name	Marks
I	ALGEBRA(Cont.)	10
II	GEOMETRY(Cont.)	9
III	TRIGONOMETRY(Cont.)	7
IV	MENSURATION(Cont.)	6
V	STATISTICS & PROBABILITY(Cont.)	8
	Total	40
	Internal Assessment	10
	Total	50

COURSE STRUCTURE TERM I

INTERNAL ASSESSMENT	Marks	TOTAL MARKS
Periodic Tests	3	
Multiple Assessments	2	10 marks for the term
Portfolio	2	
Student Enrichment Activities-practical work	3	

INTERNAL ASSESSMENT TERM II

.UNIT-ALGEBRA
1. QUADRATIC EQUATIONS (10 Periods)

Standard form of a quadratic equation $ax2 + bx + c = 0$, $(a \neq 0)$. Solutions of quadratic equations (only real roots) by factorization, and by using quadratic formula. Relationship between discriminant and nature of roots. Situational problems based on quadratic equations related to day to day activities (problems on equations reducible to quadratic equations are excluded)

2. ARITHMETIC PROGRESSIONS

Motivation for studying Arithmetic Progression Derivation of the nth term and sum of the first n terms of A.P. and their application in solving daily life problems. (Applications based on sum to n terms of an A.P. are excluded)

UNIT- GEOMETRY
3. CIRCLES

Tangent to a circle at, point of contact

1. (Prove) The tangent at any point of a circle is perpendicular to the radius through the point of contact.

2. (Prove) The lengths of tangents drawn from an external point to a circle are equal.

4. CONSTRUCTIONS

1. Division of a line segment in a given ratio (internally).

2. Tangents to a circle from a point outside it.

UNIT-TRIGONOMETRY

5. SOME APPLICATIONS OF TRIGONOMETRY

HEIGHTS AND DISTANCES-Angle of elevation, Angle of Depression. Simple problems on heights and distances. Problems should not involve more than two right triangles. Angles of elevation / depression should be only 30°, 45°, 60°.

UNIT-MENSURATION

6. SURFACE AREAS AND VOLUMES

1. Surface areas and volumes of combinations of any two of the following: cubes, cuboids, spheres, hemispheres and right circular cylinders/cones.

2. Problems involving converting one type of metallic solid into another and other mixed problems. (Problems with combination of not more than two different solids be taken).

UNIT-STATISTICS & PROBABILITY

7. STATISTICS

Mean, median and mode of grouped data (bimodal situation to be avoided). Mean by Direct Method and Assumed Mean Method only.

FOR MATHEMATICS, STUDENTS WILL ALSO BE PROVIDED WITH NCERT EXEMPLAR.

SEVEN

SCIENCE SYLLABUS TERM II

General Instructions:

1. The total Theory Examinations (Term I+II) will be of 80 marks and 20 marks weightage shall be for Internal Assessment (Term I+II).

2. Internal Assessment - Maximum Marks 10 for each Term:

a. There will be Periodic Assessment that would include:

• Three periodic tests will be conducted by the school in the entire session. Average of the two periodic tests/marks of best periodic Test conducted in the Term is to be taken for consideration.

• Diverse methods of assessment as per the need of the class dynamics and curriculum transaction. These may include - short tests, oral test, quiz, concept maps, projects, posters, presentations, enquiry based scientific investigations etc.

b. Subject Enrichment in the form of Practical/Laboratory work should be done throughout the year and the student should maintain record of the same. Practical Assessment should be continuous. All practicals listed in the syllabus must be completed.

c. Portfolio to be prepared by the student- This would include class work and other sample of student work.

Course Structure for CBSE Class 10 Science Term II

Units		Marks
I	Chemical Substances-Nature and Behaviour: Chapters 4 and 5	10
II	World of Living: Chapters 8 and 9	13
IV	Effects of Current: Chapter 12 and 13	12
V	Natural Resources: Chapter 15	05
	Total	40
	Internal Assessment	10
	Total	50

Course Structure for CBSE Class 10 Science Term II

Theme: Materials
Unit I: Chemical Substances - Nature and Behaviour
Chapter – 4 Carbon and its compounds

Carbon compounds: Covalent bonding in carbon compounds. Versatile nature of carbon. Homologous series.

Chapter – 5 Periodic classification of elements

Periodic classification of elements: Need for classification, early attempts at classification of elements (Dobereiner's Triads, Newland's Law of Octaves, Mendeleev's Periodic Table), Modern periodic table, gradation in properties, valency, atomic number, metallic and non-metallic properties.

Theme: The World of the Living
Unit II: World of Living
Chapter – 8 How do organisms reproduce?

Reproduction: Reproduction in animals and plants (asexual and sexual) reproductive health-need and methods of family planning. Safe sex vs HIV/AIDS. Child bearing and women's health.

Chapter – 9 Heredity and Evolution

Heredity: Heredity; Mendel's contribution- Laws for inheritance of traits: Sex determination: brief introduction;

Theme: Natural Phenomena
Unit IV: Effects of Current

Chapter – 12 Electricity

Ohm's law; Resistance, Resistivity, Factors on which the resistance of a conductor depends. Series combination of resistors, parallel combination of resistors and its applications in daily life. Heating effect of electric current and its applications in daily life. Electric power, Interrelation between P, V, I and R.

Chapter – 13 Magnetic effects of current

Magnetic effects of current: Magnetic field, field lines, field due to a current carrying conductor, field due to current carrying coil or solenoid; Force on current carrying conductor, Fleming's Left Hand Rule, Electric Motor, Electromagnetic induction. Induced potential difference, Induced current. Fleming's Right Hand Rule.

Theme: Natural Resources
Unit V: Natural Resources

Chapter – 15 Our Environment

Our environment: Eco-system, Environmental problems, Ozone depletion, waste production and their solutions. Biodegradable and non-biodegradable substances.

ONLY FOR INTERNAL ASSESSMENT

Note: Learners are assigned to read the below listed part of Unit V. They can be encouraged to prepare a brief write up on any one concept of this Unit in their Portfolio. This may be an assessment for Internal Assessment and credit may be given (Periodic assessment/Portfolio). This portion of the Unit is not to be assessed in the year-end examination.

Chapter – 16 Management of natural resources:

Conservation and judicious use of natural resources. Forest and wild life; Coal and Petroleum conservation. Examples of people's participation for conservation of natural resources. Big dams: advantages and limitations; alternatives, if any. Water harvesting. Sustainability of natural resources

PRACTICALS

Practical should be conducted alongside the concepts taught in theory classes.

LIST OF EXPERIMENTS

1. Studying the dependence of potential difference (V) across a resistor on the current (I) passing through it and determining its resistance. Also plotting a graph between V and I. Unit-IV:(Chapter-12)

2. Studying (a) binary fission in Amoeba, and (b) budding in yeast and Hydra with the help of prepared slides. Unit-II:(Chapter-8)

Competencies	Marks
Demonstrate Knowledge and Understanding	46%
Application of Knowledge/Concepts	22%
Analyze, Evaluate and Create	32%

Class X Science (086) Assessment Areas (Theory)

Note:
- Internal choice would be provided.
- Internal Assessment – Term II (10 Marks each)

Components of Internal Assessment

Periodic Assessment - 03 marks

Multiple Assessment – 02 marks

Subject Enrichment (Practical Work) - 03 marks

Portfolio - 02 marks

EIGHT

SOCIAL SCIENCE SYLLABUS TERM II

Unit-wise weightage for the Term 2 Exam is mentioned below:

No.	Units	No. of Periods	Marks
I	India and the Contemporary World -II	34	10
II	Contemporary India – II	19	10
III	Democratic Politics – II	14	10
IV	Economics	22	10
	Total	89	40

UNIT WISE MARKS WEIGHTAGE

COURSE CONTENT - Class 10th Term 2
TERM- II
Unit 1: India and the Contemporary World – II

Section 1: Events and Processes

2. Nationalism in India

- The First World War, Khilafat and Non - Cooperation
- Differing Strands within the Movement
- Towards Civil Disobedience
- The Sense of Collective Belonging

Section 2: Livelihoods, Economies and Societies

Note: Any one theme of the following. The theme selected should be assessed in the periodic test only and will not be evaluated in the board examination:

3. The Making of a Global World

- The Pre-modern world
- The Nineteenth Century (1815-1914)
- The Inter war Economy
- Rebuilding a World Economy: The Post-War Era

4. The Age of Industrialization

- Before the Industrial Revolution
- Hand Labour and Steam Power
- Industrialization in the colonies
- Factories Come Up
- The Peculiarities of Industrial Growth
- Market for Goods

Unit 2: Contemporary India – II

5. Minerals and Energy Resources

- What is a mineral?
- Mode of occurrence of Minerals
- Ferrous and Non-Ferrous Minerals
- Non-Metallic Minerals
- Rock Minerals
- Conservation of Minerals
- Energy Resources
- Conventional and Non-Conventional
- Conservation of Energy Resources

Note: The theoretical aspect of chapter 'Minerals and Energy Resources' to be assessed in the Periodic Tests only and will not be evaluated in Board Examination. However, the map items of this chapter as given in the Map List will be evaluated in Board Examination

6. Manufacturing Industries

- Importance of manufacturing
- Contribution of Industry to National Economy
- Industrial Location
- Classification of Industries
- Spatial distribution
- Industrial pollution and environmental degradation
- Control of Environmental Degradation

7. Life Lines of National Economy

- Transport – Roadways, Railways, Pipelines, Waterways, Airways
- Communication
- International Trade
- Tourism as a Trade

Unit 3: Democratic Politics – II

6. Political Parties

- Why do we need Political Parties?
- How many Parties should we have?
- National Political Parties
- State Parties
- Challenges to Political Parties
- How can Parties be reformed?

7. Outcomes of Democracy

- How do we assess democracy's outcomes?
- Accountable, responsive and legitimate government
- Economic growth and development
- Reduction of inequality and poverty
- Accommodation of social diversity
- Dignity and freedom of the citizens

Unit 4: Economics

3. Money and Credit

- Money as a medium of exchange

- Modern forms of money
- Loan activities of Banks
- Two different credit situations
- Terms of credit
- Formal sector credit in India
- Self Help Groups for the Poor

4. Globalization and the Indian Economy

- Production across countries
- Interlinking production across countries
- Foreign Trade and integration of markets
- What is globalization?
- Factors that have enabled Globalization
- World Trade Organization
- Impact of Globalization on India
- The Struggle for a fair Globalization

LIST OF MAP ITEMS CLASS X TERM – II

A. HISTORY (Outline Political Map of India)

Chapter - 2 Nationalism in India – (1918 – 1930) for Locating and Labelling / Identification

1. Indian National Congress Sessions:

a. Calcutta (Sep. 1920)

b. Nagpur (Dec. 1920)

c. Madras (1927)

2. Important Centres of Indian National Movement

a. Champaran (Bihar) - Movement of Indigo Planters

b. Kheda (Gujarat) - Peasant Satyagrah

c. Ahmedabad (Gujarat) - Cotton Mill Workers Satyagraha

d. Amritsar (Punjab) - Jallianwala Bagh Incident

e. Chauri Chaura (U.P.) - Calling off the Non-Cooperation Movement

f. Dandi (Gujarat) - Civil Disobedience Movement

B. GEOGRAPHY (Outline Political Map of India)

Chapter 5: Minerals and Energy Resources Power Plants- (Locating and Labelling only)

a. Thermal

· Namrup

· Singrauli

· Ramagundam

b. Nuclear

· Narora

· Kakrapara

· Tarapur

· Kalpakkam

Chapter 6: Manufacturing Industries (Locating and Labelling Only)

Cotton Textile Industries:

a. Mumbai

b. Indore

c. Surat

d. Kanpur

e. Coimbatore

Iron and Steel Plants:

a. Durgapur

b. Bokaro

c. Jamshedpur

d. Bhilai

e. Vijaynagar

f. Salem

Software Technology Parks:

a. Noida

b. Gandhinagar

c. Mumbai

d. Pune

e. Hyderabad

f. Bengaluru

g. Chennai

h. Thiruvananthapuram

Chapter 7: Lifelines of National Economy

Major Ports: (Locating and Labelling)

a. Kandla

b. Mumbai

c. Marmagao

d. New Mangalore

e. Kochi

f. Tuticorin

g. Chennai

h. Vishakhapatnam

i. Paradip

j. Haldia

International Airports:

a. Amritsar (Raja Sansi)

b. Delhi (Indira Gandhi International)

c. Mumbai (Chhatrapati Shivaji)

d. Chennai (Meenam Bakkam)

e. Kolkata (Netaji Subhash Chandra Bose)

f. Hyderabad (Rajiv Gandhi)

INTERNAL ASSESSMENT

	Marks	Description
Periodic Assessment	10 Marks	<table><tr><td>Pen Paper Test</td><td>**5 marks**</td></tr><tr><td>Assessment using multiple strategies For example, Quiz, Debate, Role Play, Viva, Group Discussion, Visual Expression, Interactive Bulletin Boards, Gallery Walks, Exit Cards, Concept Maps, Peer Assessment, Self-Assessment, etc.</td><td>**5 marks**</td></tr></table>
Portfolio	5 Marks	• Classwork and Assignments • Any exemplary work done by the student • Reflections, Narrations, Journals, etc. • Achievements of the student in the subject throughout the year • Participation of the student in different activities like Heritage India Quiz
Subject Enrichment Activity	5 Marks	• Project Work
TOTAL	**20 MARKS**	

INTERNAL ASSESSMENT TERM II

PROJECT WORK

05 Marks

1. Every student has to compulsorily undertake any one project on the following topics:

Consumer Awareness

OR

Social Issues

OR

Sustainable Development

2. Objective: The overall objective of the project work is to help students gain an insight and pragmatic understanding of the theme

and see all the Social Science disciplines from interdisciplinary perspective. It should also help in enhancing the Life Skills of the students.

Students are expected to apply the Social Science concepts that they have learnt over the years in order to prepare the project report.

If required, students may go out for collecting data and use different primary and secondary resources to prepare the project. If possible, different forms of Art may be integrated in the project work.

3. The distribution of marks over different aspects relating to Project Work is as follows:

S. No.	Aspects	Marks
a.	Content accuracy, originality and analysis	2
b.	Presentation and creativity	2
c.	Viva Voce	1

PROJECT EVALUATION

4. The projects carried out by the students in different topics should subsequently be shared among themselves through interactive sessions such as exhibitions, panel discussions, etc.

5. All documents pertaining to assessment under this activity should be meticulously maintained by concerned schools.

6. A Summary Report should be prepared highlighting:

→ objectives realized through individual work and group interactions;

→ calendar of activities;

→ innovative ideas generated in the process (like comic strips, drawings, illustrations, script play etc.);

→ list of questions asked in viva voce.

7. It is to be noted here by all the teachers and students that the projects and models prepared should be made from eco-friendly products without incurring too much expenditure.

8. The Project Report should be handwritten by the students themselves.

9. Records pertaining to projects (internal assessment) of the students will be maintained for a period of three months from the date of declaration of result for verification at the discretion of Board. Subjudiced cases, if any or those involving RTI / Grievances may however be retained beyond three months.

NINE

MATHEMATICS-Standard QUESTION PAPER DESIGN

S.No.	Typology of Questions	Total Marks	% Weightage
1	**Remembering:** Exhibit memory of previously learned material by recalling facts, terms, basic concepts, and answers. **Understanding:** Demonstrate understanding of facts and ideas by organizing, comparing, translating, interpreting, giving descriptions, and stating main ideas	43	54
2	**Applying:** Solve problems to new situations by applying acquired knowledge, facts, techniques and rules in a different way.	19	24
3	**Analysing :** Examine and break information into parts by identifying motives or causes. Make inferences and find evidence to support generalizations **Evaluating:** Present and defend opinions by making judgments about information, validity of ideas, or quality of work based on a set of criteria. **Creating:** Compile information together in a different way by combining elements in a new pattern or proposing alternative solutions	18	22
	Total	80	100

MATHEMATICS BLUEPRINT

TEN

SCIENCE TOPOLOGY

Note:

- Typology of Questions: VSA including objective type questions, Assertion – Reasoning type questions;
- SA; LA; Source-based/ Case-based/ Passage-based/ Integrated assessment questions.
- An internal choice of approximately 33% would be provided.

Internal Assessment (20 Marks)

- Periodic Assessment – 05 marks + 05 marks
- Subject Enrichment (Practical Work) – 05 marks
- Portfolio – 05 marks

Suggestive verbs for various competencies

- Demonstrate Knowledge and Understanding
- State, name, list, identify, define, suggest, describe, outline, summarize, etc.
- Application of Knowledge/Concepts
- Calculate, illustrate, show, adapt, explain, distinguish, etc.

- Analyze, Evaluate and Create
- Interpret, analyze, compare, contrast, examine, evaluate, discuss, construct, etc

ELEVEN

ENGLISH COMPETENCIES

Sections	Competencies	Total Marks	% Weightage
Reading Comprehension	Conceptual understanding, decoding, analyzing, inferring, interpreting and vocabulary	20	25%
Writing Skill and Grammar	Creative expression of an opinion, reasoning, justifying, illustrating, appropriacy of style and tone, using appropriate format and fluency. Applying conventions, using integrated structures with accuracy and fluency	20	25%
Literature Textbook and Supplementary Reading Text	Recalling, reasoning, appreciating, applying literary conventions illustrating and justifying etc. Extract relevant information, identifying the central theme and sub-theme, understanding the writers' message and writing fluently.	40	50%
Total		80	

PAPER PATTERN

Section	Topics	Weightage
1	Reading Skills	30
2	Writing Skills with Grammar	20
3	Literature Textbook and Supplementary Reading Text	30
	Total	80

BASED ON SECTIONS

TWELVE

SOCIAL SCIENCE STRUCTURE

SYLLABUS STD 10

S.No.	Competencies	Total marks	% Weightage
1	**Remembering and Understanding:** Exhibiting memory of previously learned material by recalling facts, terms, basic concepts, and answers; Demonstrating understanding of facts and ideas by organizing, comparing, translating, interpreting, giving descriptions and stating main ideas	28	35%
2	**Applying:** Solving problems to new situations by applying acquired knowledge, facts, techniques and rules in a different way	15	18.75%
3	**Formulating, Analysing, Evaluating and Creating:** Examining and breaking information into parts by identifying motives or causes; Making inferences and finding evidence to support generalizations; Presenting and defending opinions by making judgments about information, validity of ideas, or quality of work based on a set of criteria; Compiling information together in a different way by combining elements in a new pattern or proposing alternative solutions.	32	40%
4	Map Skill	5	6.25%
		80	100%

TYPE QUESTIONS

THIRTEEN
OVERALL VIEW

Total Number of Lessons to be studied in the Academic Year 2022-23

Subject	Total Lessons
English	21
Mathematics	15
Science	16
Social Science	25
Total Lessons	**77**
Excluding Grammar and Writing Skills for English. They will be taught but is not included in this count.	

Total Number of Month wise Working Days

Month	Working Days	Total Weekend Test
April	26	4
May	**Complete Off**	
June	26	4
July	26	5
August	26	4
September	26	4
October	22	4
November	26	4
December	25	4
January	25	5
February	24	4
March	**Final Examination Revision**	
Total	254	42

List of Holidays:
15th August: Independence Day
22nd October to 26th October: Diwali Vacations
26th January: Republic Day
Class Duration: 2 Hours Per Day
Timings will be decided with your consent.
Note that there are many tests planned based on JEE | NEET Pattern as well. All Month End Tests will follow JEE | NEET | MH-CET Test Patterns.

First Weekend Tests (MCQ) will be conducted online on Heavenly Blessings Mobile Application to provide the practise of CPT pattern.

Second Weekend Test (Subjective) will be conducted offline.

Third Weekend Test (MCQ) will be conducted online on Heavenly Blessings Mobile Application based on JEE | NEET | MH-CET Pattern.

Fourth Weekend Test (subjective) will be conducted offline. Subject will be informed timely.

"WE WILL ALSO CONDUCT TESTS BASED ON PREVIOUS YEAR CBSE QUESTION PAPERS IN THE MONTH OF MARCH."

www.ingramcontent.com/pod-product-compliance
Lightning Source LLC
Chambersburg PA
CBHW060911130726
48001CB00006B/2197